# Instrumental Solos for TENOR SAX

# RODGERS AND HAMMERSTEIN™

# THE SOUND OF MUSIC

## How To Use The CD Accompaniment:
A melody cue appears on the right channel only. If your CD player has a balance adjustment,
you can adjust the volume of the melody by turning down the right channel.

ISBN 0-634-02726-3

**WILLIAMSON MUSIC®**

A RODGERS AND HAMMERSTEIN COMPANY

www.williamsonmusic.com

EXCLUSIVELY DISTRIBUTED BY

**HAL•LEONARD®**
CORPORATION

7777 W. BLUEMOUND RD. P.O. BOX 13819 MILWAUKEE, WI 53213

Visit Hal Leonard Online at
**www.halleonard.com**

The offering of this publication for sale is not to be construed as authorization for the performance of any material contained herein.
Applications for the right to perform THE SOUND OF MUSIC, in whole or in part, could be addressed to
The Rodgers & Hammerstein Theatre Library
229 West 28th Street, 11th Floor
New York, NY 10001
Tel: 800/400.8160 or 212/564.400 • Fax: 212/268.1245.
E-mail: theatre@rnh.com • Website: www.rnh.com

# RODGERS AND HAMMERSTEIN™
# THE SOUND OF MUSIC®

## Contents

# ◆ DO-RE-MI

**TENOR SAX**

Lyrics by OSCAR HAMMERSTEIN II
Music by RICHARD RODGERS

# ❷ THE SOUND OF MUSIC

**TENOR SAX**

Lyrics by OSCAR HAMMERSTEIN II
Music by RICHARD RODGERS

# ❸ MARIA

TENOR SAX

Lyrics by OSCAR HAMMERSTEIN II<br>
Music by RICHARD RODGERS

# ◆ MY FAVORITE THINGS

TENOR SAX

Lyrics by OSCAR HAMMERSTEIN II
Music by RICHARD RODGERS

# ◆5 EDELWEISS

TENOR SAX

Lyrics by OSCAR HAMMERSTEIN II
Music by RICHARD RODGERS

# ◆6 THE LONELY GOATHERD

TENOR SAX

Lyrics by OSCAR HAMMERSTEIN II
Music by RICHARD RODGERS

# ◆ 7 SIXTEEN GOING ON SEVENTEEN

TENOR SAX

Lyrics by OSCAR HAMMERSTEIN II
Music by RICHARD RODGERS

# ◆8 SO LONG, FAREWELL

TENOR SAX

Lyrics by OSCAR HAMMERSTEIN II
Music by RICHARD RODGERS

# ◆⑨ CLIMB EV'RY MOUNTAIN

TENOR SAX

Lyrics by OSCAR HAMMERSTEIN II
Music by RICHARD RODGERS

# PLAY ALONG CD COLLECTIONS

## BAND JAM

12 band favorites complete with accompaniment CD, including: Born to Be Wild • Danger Zone • Devil with the Blue Dress • Final Countdown • Get Ready for This • Gonna Make You Sweat (Everybody Dance Now) • I Got You (I Feel Good) • Rock & Roll - Part II (The Hey Song) • Twist and Shout • We Will Rock You • Wild Thing • Y.M.C.A.

|  |  |  |
|---|---|---|
| _____ 00841232 | Flute | $10.95 |
| _____ 00841233 | Clarinet | $10.95 |
| _____ 00841234 | Alto Sax | $10.95 |
| _____ 00841235 | Trumpet | $10.95 |
| _____ 00841236 | Horn | $10.95 |
| _____ 00841237 | Trombone | $10.95 |
| _____ 00841238 | Violin | $10.95 |

## DISNEY SOLOS – INTERMEDIATE LEVEL

An exciting collection of 12 solos with professional orchestral accompaniment on CD. Titles include: Be Our Guest • Can You Feel the Love Tonight • Colors of the Wind • Friend like Me • Under the Sea • You've Got a Friend in Me • Zero to Hero • and more.

|  |  |  |
|---|---|---|
| _____ 00841404 | Flute | $12.95 |
| _____ 00841506 | Oboe | $12.95 |
| _____ 00841405 | Clarinet/Tenor Sax | $12.95 |
| _____ 00841406 | Alto Sax | $12.95 |
| _____ 00841407 | Horn | $12.95 |
| _____ 00841408 | Trombone | $12.95 |
| _____ 00841409 | Trumpet | $12.95 |
| _____ 00841410 | Violin | $12.95 |
| _____ 00841411 | Viola | $12.95 |
| _____ 00841412 | Cello | $12.95 |
| _____ 00841553 | Mallet Percussion | $12.95 |

## EASY DISNEY FAVORITES

A fantastic selection of 13 Disney favorites for solo instuments, including: Bibbidi-Bobbidi-Boo • Candle on the Water • Chim Chim Cher-ee • A Dream Is a Wish Your Heart Makes • It's a Small World • Let's Go Fly a Kite • Mickey Mouse March • A Spoonful of Sugar • Supercalifragilisticexpialidocious • Toyland March • Winnie the Pooh • The Work Song • Zip-A-Dee-Doo-Dah. Each book features a play-along CD with complete rhythm section accompaniment.

|  |  |  |
|---|---|---|
| _____ 00841371 | Flute | $10.95 |
| _____ 00841477 | Clarinet | $10.95 |
| _____ 00841478 | Alto Sax | $10.95 |
| _____ 00841479 | Trumpet | $10.95 |
| _____ 00841480 | Trombone | $10.95 |
| _____ 00841372 | Violin | $10.95 |
| _____ 00841481 | Viola | $10.95 |
| _____ 00841482 | Cello/Bass | $10.95 |

## FAVORITE MOVIE THEMES

13 themes, including: An American Symphony from *Mr. Holland's Opus* • Braveheart • Chariots of Fire • Forrest Gump – Main Title • Theme from *Jurassic Park* • Mission: Impossible Theme • and more.

|  |  |  |
|---|---|---|
| _____ 00841166 | Flute | $10.95 |
| _____ 00841167 | Clarinet | $10.95 |
| _____ 00841169 | Alto Sax | $10.95 |
| _____ 00841168 | Trumpet/Tenor Sax | $10.95 |
| _____ 00841171 | Horn | $10.95 |
| _____ 00841170 | Trombone | $10.95 |
| _____ 00841296 | Violin | $10.95 |

## HYMNS FOR THE MASTER

15 inspirational favorites, including: All Hail the Power of Jesus' Name • Amazing Grace • Crown Him With Many Crowns • Joyful, Joyful We Adore Thee • This Is My Father's World • When I Survey the Wondrous Cross • and more.

|  |  |  |
|---|---|---|
| _____ 00841136 | Flute | $12.95 |
| _____ 00841137 | Clarinet | $12.95 |
| _____ 00841138 | Alto Sax | $12.95 |
| _____ 00841139 | Trumpet | $12.95 |
| _____ 00841140 | Trombone | $12.95 |
| _____ 00841239 | Piano Accompaniment (no CD) | $8.95 |

## JAZZ & BLUES

14 songs for solo instruments, complete with a play-along CD. Includes: Bernie's Tune • Cry Me a River • Fever • Fly Me to the Moon • God Bless' the Child • Harlem Nocturne • Moonglow • A Night in Tunisia • One Note Samba • Opus One • Satin Doll • Slightly Out of Tune (Desafinado) • Take the "A" Train • Yardbird Suite.

|  |  |  |
|---|---|---|
| 00841438 | Flute | $10.95 |
| 00841439 | Clarinet | $10.95 |
| 00841440 | Alto Sax | $10.95 |
| 00841441 | Trumpet | $10.95 |
| 00841442 | Tenor Sax | $10.95 |
| 00841443 | Trombone | $10.95 |
| 00841444 | Violin | $10.95 |

## MAMBO NO. 5, MARIA MARIA, AND OTHER LATIN HITS

These long-awaited play-along book/CD packs feature 10 super hot Latin hits: Genie in a Bottle • I Need to Know • I Wan'na Be like You (The Monkey Song) • If You Had My Love • Mambo No. 5 (A Little Bit Of...) • Mambo Swing • Maria Maria • Mucho Mambo • Para De Jugar • You Sang to Me.

|  |  |  |
|---|---|---|
| 00841526 | Flute | $10.95 |
| 00841527 | Clarinet | $10.95 |
| 00841528 | Alto Sax | $10.95 |
| 00841529 | Tenor Sax | $10.95 |
| 00841530 | Trumpet | $10.95 |
| 00841531 | Horn | $10.95 |
| 00841532 | Trombone | $10.95 |
| 00841533 | Violin | $10.95 |

## PLAY THE DUKE

Features 11 classics from Duke Ellington's stellar career: Caravan • Don't Get Around Much Anymore • I Got It Bad and That Ain't Good • I'm Beginning to See the Light • In a Sentimental Mood • It Don't Mean a Thing (If It Ain't Got That Swing) • Mood Indigo • Satin Doll • Solitude • Sophisticated Lady • Take the "A" Train.

|  |  |  |
|---|---|---|
| 00841515 | Flute | $10.95 |
| 00841516 | Clarinet | $10.95 |
| 00841517 | Alto Sax | $10.95 |
| 00841518 | Tenor Sax | $10.95 |
| 00841519 | Trumpet | $10.95 |
| 00841520 | Horn | $10.95 |
| 00841521 | Trombone | $10.95 |
| 00841522 | Violin | $10.95 |

## ROCK JAMS

12 rockin' favorites to jam along with the accompanying CD. Songs include: Addicted to Love • Another One Bites the Dust • Get Ready • Love Shack • What I Like About You • and more.

|  |  |  |
|---|---|---|
| _____ 00841251 | Flute | $10.95 |
| _____ 00841252 | Clarinet/Tenor Sax | $10.95 |
| _____ 00841253 | Alto Sax | $10.95 |
| _____ 00841254 | Trumpet | $10.95 |
| _____ 00841257 | Horn | $10.95 |
| _____ 00841255 | Trombone/Baritone | $10.95 |
| _____ 00841256 | Violin | $10.95 |

**FROM**

FOR MORE INFORMATION, SEE YOUR LOCAL MUSIC DEALER, OR WRITE TO:

## HAL•LEONARD® CORPORATION

7777 W. BLUEMOUND RD. P.O. BOX 13819 MILWAUKEE, WI 53213

http://www.halleonard.com

Prices, contents, and availability subject to change without notice.